Stock Market Investing for Beginners

A Winning Guide to Start Grow Your Money, Build Wealth and Stock Trading

by

Michael J. Bloomfield

engaging in the rendering of legal, financial, medical or professional advice. The content within this book has been derived from various sources. Please consult a licensed professional before attempting any techniques outlined in this book.

By reading this document, the reader agrees that under no circumstances is the author responsible for any losses, direct or indirect, which are incurred as a result of the use of information contained within this document, including, but not limited to, — errors, omissions, or inaccuracies.

Table Of Contents

Foreword

In any room in your home, there's a good chance you can find some pennies laying around. Instead of allowing these pennies to collect dust, why not invest them so you can produce more income without even leaving home? The stock market can scare away anyone without money or knowledge, but luckily, you don't need much of the first one, and this book will provide you with the second!

Some may be experiencing economic crisis, but there are plenty who find their funds doubling within a day - all because they understand how to invest their earnings into penny stocks. Whether you have student loans to pay off, a fund started for a house you want to add to, or something you want to buy, you can start to find financial freedom with the use of penny stocks.

There's a misconception that penny stocks are easy to navigate, but don't let that discourage you. Though they don't require much money to start, they can be sometimes risky to navigate. To ensure profit is made and a scam is avoided, you need research to make sure there aren't any mishaps. This book will lay the groundwork of what is required to become a successful penny stock investor.

The benefit of learning about penny stock is the ability to build funds with almost no money at all. The change in your pocket could turn into the fund you use to pay off your college fees, or a vacation that's well-deserved. Some people might even want to invest in penny stocks as a way to start their career. Financial freedom has never been easier, and luckily, we have the ability to do so with just a couple of coins!

This book will explain the basics behind penny stock in general while creating a basic guide filled with tips to help you navigate through your first purchase and sale. Within a week, you could be investing pennies into stocks that will turn into more and more money. It's important to know that this doesn't happen overnight, but with proper dedication and commitment to earning, money can be made by making investments that are less than a dollar. Some people make mistakes when investing by not doing their research, so tools like these are important to help investors avoid common rookie mistakes. There might be times that even the most successful investors have losses, but losing money should never be the result of not doing proper research.

The benefits of investing pennies into stock will speak for themselves once earners start seeing the numbers in their accounts go up. Anyone is capable of making investments. It starts with doing your homework to make sure that you can make the most from the change at the bottom of your bag. There is never a better time to start investing than right now! Whether you're young or old, rich or poor, reading this guide is your first step towards making more money.

Introduction

"The trick is not to learn to trust your gut feelings, but rather to discipline yourself to ignore them. Stand by your stocks as long as the fundamental story of the company hasn't changed." – Peter Lynch[1].

(Image via Pixabay)

As the title suggests, this book is going to be about the stock

---

[1] Peter Lynch is one of the most successful investors in the world. He is a former manager of the Magellan Fund, and has become a millionaire philanthropist that inspires many other investors.

market[2], specifically for beginners. However, even the greatest stock investors may find useful information in this book. A true investor knows that there is never too much information they can receive about a particular transaction.

This book will start with the basic background of penny stocks[3]. The history, development, and future predictions of penny stocks are important to understanding for anyone interested in the business. We will then take you through the steps necessary to evaluate whether something should be invested in, and how to do so once a good decision has been made.

We'll help you understand the stock market so that even a 10-year old who wants to start investing in stocks can do it! The stock market is important to our global economy, and you shouldn't fear it. Though not everyone is going to buy stock in their lifetime, anyone is capable of becoming an investor.

Disclaimer

This book is not responsible for any poor financial decisions or losses that one might incur. It simply exists as a guide for those interested in penny stocks through their investment journey. What works for one person might not work for the other. Any

---

[2] A stock market is the exchange of stock. Stock refers to a subscription of shares of a company that raise a corporation's capital.
[3] Stock that is valued at less than a dollar per share.

mistakes made while trading is not at the fault of the author of this book, or anyone else associated with its creation.

This book is not a promise that money will be made. Though there are certain success stories of those that invest with penny stocks, choosing to make these trades is not a promise that you will end up making money. More is required than reading this book to achieve financial freedom with penny stocks.

This book not liable for any investing decisions the reader takes. In no way does anyone associated with the creation of this book claim responsibility for any losses or gains from any reader that chooses to make investments after completion of the book. Any money spent, earned, lost, or otherwise is 100% the responsibility of the reader.

Chapter 1 – Introduction to the Stock Market

Before getting into penny stocks, it's important to have a general knowledge of stocks. Whether you're here as someone who's already invested and wants to look into penny stocks, or someone that has no idea what stock even means, by the end of the book you'll have a comprehensive knowledge of what it takes to make money from the stock market.

Some people get into stocks as a way to make a little extra money. Others have the capabilities to turn this into their fulltime job. Many people struggle with student debt, rent that's too high, and other frequent problems with money. These issues can be debilitating. Luckily, stocks help you make money from the pennies you already have.

A stock market is all the buyers and sellers of stocks in one collection. The stocks are representative of interests owned in certain companies. Some stocks are private while others are publicly traded. Some automatically go to the New York Stock Exchange when they start thinking of stocks, but that's just one example.

Companies put their stocks into exchanges to liquify[4] their shares. Investors love this liquidity so much so that foreign investors become interested as well. The Global Stock Market

---

[4] Something that can be liquified can easily be traded for cash.

has an estimated worth of $76.3 trillion! The NYSE[5] alone is $21 trillion of that massive fortune.

Before getting more into the stock exchange now, it's important to understand the history.

History

(Image via Pixabay)

The stock market plays an important role in today's global

---

[5] NYSE stands for "New York Stock Exchange," the largest stock market in the world, located in New York City.

14

economy, but it hasn't always been around. Now, there are many countries that actually depend on various stock markets to achieve economic growth. Although it's so important, the stock market is fairly new in world history.

Stock markets started appearing in the 1500s, though there were other kinds of economic systems around before that were similar. The general consensus is that the stock market system appeared in Antwerp, the commercial center of Belgium. This first system didn't involve trading shares in a company, and instead relied on individual debt, businesses, and the affairs of the Government.

At one point, there was a ban on issuing shares, but the London Stock Exchange soon appeared in 1801. By 1825, companies were legally allowed to issue shares. If this ban had not been there, the London Stock Exchange might have become a "global superpower" instead of the NYSE.

The NYSE popped up in 1817, and history has not been the same. It wasn't the first in the country, but it has become the most important. Not only has the NYSE become vital in the country's economic structures, but to maintaining global economics as well.

The 2008 Crisis

On September 16, 2008, there was an economic crisis that caused many countries to close their stock markets. This was only temporary, but it was a financial disaster that's still greatly affecting global economics. The mishap was due to the exposure of subprime loans, and the resulting credit default swaps that were issued to protect these loans as well as their issuers.

This crisis affected many global markets negatively, including markets in Iceland, London, and Indonesia. Many markets were suspended for days at a time, causing different shares to drop greatly in value. Some believed it wasn't as bad as others, while certain people believe this time in 2008 was the greatest financial crisis in world history. We can't know for certain as many people are still suffering from the negative effects.

No matter how much damage this actually caused, it's still a terrifying case of what could happen if things go wrong. While there is a scary risk when it comes to the stock market, nevertheless there are still plenty of people who have found success by trading different stocks.

A Notable Case

Tim Grittani is now a millionaire who was able to make his fortune by trading penny stocks. He started by purchasing OTC stocks, which were ones that were being pumped and dumped by their promoters. This "Pump and dump" scheme can be dangerous, and we'll discuss its potential harmful factors later in the book.

This kind of stock is so successful because they might go up 100-s percentage points in a day, but they can also drop by 50% after they have been run up. To actually turn a profit from these, you have to be a very skilled trader. Luckily, Tim was able to do this with practice and knowledge that it took to make sure he wasn't getting scammed.

Many pumps and dump schemes are illegal, so there aren't as many around today. Tim Grittani still trades, but instead of penny stocks, his focus is on bigger trades in the Nasdaq[6] stocks. It wasn't easy in the beginning, but Tim Grittani is an example of what can happen if you're knowledgeable, dedicated, and passionate about what it is that you plan to do to make a huge fortune in penny stocks.

---

[6] Nasdaq is a method of using a quick and computerized way to trade stock. It was developed in 1971 by the National Association of Securities Dealers.

The Future of Stocks

The FAANGs has become a great concern for those invested in stock today. FAANG stands for Facebook, Apple, Amazon, Netflix, and Google. These massive companies play a huge role in the stock market, and when there's so much power in one company, there can be so much more of a negative consequence should something go wrong.

The FAANGs make up at least an eight of the total value of the S&P 500 Index[7]. They have also accounted for at least half of the market's growth, just this year. This has caused the stock market to become very dependent on these few companies alone. For the future of the stock market, we can only assume that these businesses will become much more powerful. The more money invested, the higher they will grow. The higher they grow, the farther they'll fall should something happen. It can be a scary time when looking at the stock market, but it can also be one of hope and profit.

---

[7] S&P 500 Index is an index of the 500 largest U.S. companies that are publicly traded. It is organized by the market value and is market-capitalization-weighted.

Fundamentals

A market fundamental[8], which is also known as a fundamental value, is associated with the stream of future cash flows that are attached to the asset at it's discounted present value. Market fundamentals determine the asset prices, and so the value of that asset is positively dependent on future cash flows that are expected. It depends negatively on the present value and the discount rate used to obtain that. Market fundamentals and values move together. However, market fundamentals might tend to exhibit a lower volatility, which leads to many conclude asset prices deviate from their fundamental values.

There is another component of these market fundamentals of different stocks, which is the discount rate that was used to obtain a present value of these dividends[9]. You might expect that a market fundamental decreases due to the discount rate being higher, because of the fixed stream of cash flows cause an increase in the expected future returns. It's important to remember, however, that individual stocks and their expected returns, as well as the stock market as a whole, are not constant. There are many different macroeconomic variables

---

[8] Market Fundamental is the basic fundamental qualities of a particular company. Fundamentals include looking at a business's operation, management, media attention, customers, need, and other basic traits that make up a company.
[9] Dividends refer to the payments made from a corporation to the shareholders of a certain stock. Sometimes, stock shares might be distributed to shareholders in place of a cash payment.

that hold various information that could forecast returns.

Investing

(Image via Pixabay)

You are reading this book with a wish to solve your money problems. It is true that your life can certainly be changed with stocks. Your financial future is dependent on acquiring financial freedom as soon as possible. Investing in stocks can certainly help.

There are some stocks that are growing at a faster rate than their industry's average. This growth is most commonly seen in fast-growing industries with the potential to give the shareholders a return actually greater than what is offered from the stocks of companies that are a part of older and more established industries. Though these have high returns, these growth stocks are the most volatile, and they are just as likely to go down in price as they are to go up.

You have many options in investing your money when it comes to different stocks. You could choose value stocks[10], which are good earning stocks that have high growth potential. These value stocks sell at a low price that is relative to their actual value. Income stocks are another option, but these stocks aren't expected to grow that much in their share price. They still pay consistently when it comes to their dividends. Blue-Chip[11] stocks are the largest and are associated with well-known companies that have great reputations, as well as records of strong profit growth.

Penny stocks can sometimes be the riskiest investment. However, they are the only option for those that don't have as much money to invest in, for example, blue-chip stocks. Penny stocks are associated with companies that might have erratic and short histories of performance. Penny stocks sell for $5 or less for every share.

---

[10] Value stock refers to company shares in which the fundamental aspects are less than competitors, usually determined after all aspects of value are analyzed.
[11] Blue-chip refers to high-quality products and services. Blue-chip stock is among the highest priced, but also highest quality, stock that a person could buy. It is derivative of the highest chip in poker, the blue-chip.

Stock is an important concept for everyone to learn, but it's especially important that we start teaching our children as well. They are future investors, and the sooner they can understand the concept of trading stock, the better equipped they'll be when it comes to making their own money and investing in their own children's future as well.

There are a few apps that can help teach your children how to invest in stocks. For adult beginners, there's no shame in using these apps for yourself either.

Stockpile helps kids to invest in companies that they actually care about, such as Disney and Apple. By using logos and companies that children are familiar with, it helps to get them excited about the companies they would normally otherwise ignore.

Busy Kid is another app that not only helps teach stocks, but about money in general. It allows parents to input allowance amounts, suggesting chores to go along with this too. Kids can say right in the app when they've completed a chore, and they'll soon get their allowance. They can then use this money to cash out, purchase gift cards, donate, or even invest.

Chapter 2 – Why Penny Stocks?

(Image via Pixabay)

Penny stocks have the potential to give massive returns, but they can also come with a risk. Why might you choose to invest in penny stocks when they are so many other options? There are two main reasons why you should choose to invest in penny stocks, but it's important to ensure that you understand what penny stocks are before getting into the benefits.

A penny stock isn't exactly what it sounds like. You can't start investing with just one penny. Usually, these stocks are a few dollars, usually less than $5. Penny stocks use Pink Sheets[12], FINRA[13]'s OTC Bulletin Board, also referred to as OTCBB[14].

---

[12] A pink sheet is a publication created by the National Quotation Bureau. It is released on a daily basis and exhibits OTC stock bids and ask prices, as well as the investors that are doing the exchanging.
[13] FINRA stands for The Financial Industry Regulatory Authority. This is an independent security firm that conducts regulatory business in the United States.

Pink Sheets can sometimes be dangerous, as companies are not required by the Securities and Exchange Commission, also known as SEC[15], to file. There are no minimum standards in place for a company to list their stocks on these Pink Sheets or the OTCBB. Because of this, there can be some scammers that take advantage of investors.

While the risks are certainly present, it's not always as scary to invest as these stocks have a low price and a high return potential. Of course, you should never invest more than what you're OK with losing, so only those who get too excited and spend all their money on Penny Stocks will be the ones to suffer in the end.

They are responsible for regulating securities, which refer to the financial industries that are traded among different free stock markets.

[14] OTCBB stands for over-the-counter bulletin board, which is a digital trading service, also provided by NASD, in which investors and traders can have consistent quotes of different stock, giving insight into up-to-date stock information.

[15] SEC stands for Securities and Exchange Commission; an agency of the U.X. Government that is responsible for monitoring securities transactions, as well as the activities of investors and traders in the attempt to prevent scams, fraud, and any other illegal activity.

Low Price

There is certainly a potential to become wealthy when it comes to investing in penny stocks. Most people who are ready to invest have to start small, watching as a company grows large. Penny stocks are a great place to start, as the prices can be very low in the beginning. If nothing goes anywhere, not as much money is lost because shares were purchased at such a low cost.

To start investing in penny stocks, you must be ready to lose everything. There are going to be moments of loss, but it isn't as detrimental with penny stocks because it might be an amount less than $50 total. That is why many people choose to invest in these penny stocks versus blue-chip stocks that might cause the investors to lose thousands or more.

While there is a chance of losing out on money, there's a great chance to have a high return potential as well. The key to making sure that even your pennies don't go to waste is by looking for companies that have a high future growth potential. Figuring out what might cause this will be discussed later in the book.

High Return Potential

Penny stocks are incredibly inexpensive, but have the chance of giving a high return potential. Even the biggest stocks also affect penny stocks, which means that there is a chance when things are going well for others, they'll be doing great for penny stocks as well. Just in the same breath, a crash for big blue-chip stocks will certainly negatively affect penny stocks as well. No one is safe from an economic crisis, but penny stocks have less of a loss.

These stocks can be the greatest type of investment. There's no business upkeep, hiring of employees, or clocking into the office every day. All it takes is a few dollars, and with the right knowledge, you have the potential to take home millions.

Chapter 3 – Trading Analysis

(Image via Pixabay)

A trading analysis is incredibly important for you to succeed in trading penny stocks. This chapter is the beginning of the important information that actually provides solutions. At this point, you should have a decent understanding of what stock is and how penny stock differs from the rest. The consequences, risks, and returns will be discussed later, but it's still important to make sure that penny stock is understood at this point. If not, refer to the glossary at the end of the book.

Penny stocks can sometimes be challenging to research, as they are usually less than a dollar in price and can be very thinly traded. What also makes penny stocks different is that they don't require the same reports that other larger stocks do, and they don't have consistent oversight. Because penny stocks lack both of these, they have the potential to be more dangerous than others.

On some days, penny stocks have the potential to have price swings of over twenty percent. This is pretty common as well, so to ensure that investing in penny stocks won't get you in any trouble, a thorough analysis is encouraged. There are a few ways to conduct these analyses to make sure that investors aren't going to run into money issues continually.

Fundamental Analysis

Fundamentals were mentioned in the first chapter. Fundamental analysis is important to determine which stock is going to be winning, and which should be avoided. The most important aspects of fundamental analysis include e-finance, microeconomics, news trading, financial statement research, company research, and industry research.

Fundamental analysis is a study of all of the facts surrounding a company and its history. This analysis will look into all the things that encompass a company within its sector, as well as in the broader market. A fundamental analysis will look at the data involved with a company's products, how these products are developed, the intellectual property that surrounds the product including patents, as well as the management, finances, and competition.

When looking at whether or not a company is successful and should be invested in, these factors all need to be researched. If there are any faults or downsides that might seem risky, an investor wouldn't want to put their money towards this particular company.

Some other factors that are also important to study in a fundamental analysis include:

- Industry

- Currency

- Media

- Investors, alliances, and public support

- Market and current economy

- Trends and marketeer involvement

- And many more

The key to doing a proper fundamental analysis is looking at every aspect of a company before investing. You can't just pick out a company you like and put your money on that. You have to consider if it's the right time economically, who are involved in helping the company thrive, and the media surrounding the current trends involved in that company. If a news story hits about a certain lip gloss causing people's faces to breakout, you wouldn't want to invest in that even if they own all the different varieties of the gloss.

Technical Analysis

A technical analysis will look at stock tables to understand the financial potential of a certain share. These trading charts are important to look at, as they give clues to the direction of future stock prices. A technical analysis might be more reliable for bigger companies that have consistent trends. However, they're still crucial for penny stocks as well.

Support and resistances of a trading chart will help determine where a company might be going. Support is a price level that helps show when demand is strong enough to keep the price from declining further. Resistance is a point at which the price level has become strong enough to prevent the price from rising further.

(Image via Pixabay)

Candle patterns[16] in trading charts might have the potential to predict certain movements. It is a pattern in the movement of prices that looks like a candlestick, with the "wick" determining which way a price might go.

There are many chart patterns that show different trading indicators that could help you know whether or not you should be putting your money towards a certain share. A technical analysis aims to remind you that you aren't investing in a company, rather, getting what you can from a particular share. Penny stocks are short and quick, so knowing how to read trading charts isn't always going to tell you whether or not you

---

[16] Candle patterns refer to a movement seen among trading charts in which the pattern represents a candlestick. These movements might have the ability to predict a market movement, helping investors know whether or not they are making a good decision.

should put your money towards a share.

Even experts may have trouble reading trading charts. It's important to remember that they will all always include the price and volume of a share. When reading a trade chart, look at what the bars are indicating about price and time. An investor must indicate both of these to ensure that they are putting their money in the right place. By this point, you should have a basic understanding of how to read trade charts, but the only way to get good at it is by actually reading real trade charts. The more you can get your hands on, the better. By evaluating many different trading charts and looking at the patterns of shares, you can better understand whether or not to put your money towards a share when you find a trading chart that seems reliable.

Finding the Right Stocks

The easiest way that you can find penny stocks to put your money towards is to use stock charts. You should be well versed in reading stock charts to find patterns that are reliable and help determine what a stock might do next. You can't find the right stock based on the technical analysis[17] alone, however.

---

[17] Technical Analysis is an analysis of a company looking at the numbers father than the fundamental aspects of what makes up that business.

You also have to make sure that you're looking at a fundamental analysis[18] and everything that might go into making sure that a particular product is the one that should be invested in.

The first place to look for penny stocks is on Pink Sheets and the OTCBB. There is an endless amount of penny stocks that you can invest in, so a good place to start is with a company that you actually know something about. Maybe it's your favorite grocery store, or a product you use every day. Not everything we use can be invested in, but the more familiar you are with a company, the better.

Next, look at what's currently happening with that company. Is it about to be purchased by someone else, or is there a big change in the company's direction that's going to affect how much money is being made?

Once a fundamental analysis has been conducted, it's time to look at the charts. Look for something that seems to be already growing, just a bit, in the value. If there's a little bit of a trend that's rising, jump on it. Don't do so if the chart seems to be already peaking, however. It has to be right when the company is starting to grow.

---

[18] Fundamental analysis is a method of evaluating a stock to determine the value. A fundamental analysis includes looking at a company's fundamental pars, such as status, marketing, affiliates, and other relevant parts of the company to determine the value. This differs from a technical analysis, which looks more into the numbers.

Some stocks might go up simply because someone invested more into them. Someone putting $100,000 to a million dollars into a stock, they raise it themselves, which is a tactic some people do. The better you can evaluate whether or not a stock is the right one for you, the better you'll be able to make a profit from the money that you put in.

Chapter 4 – How to Trade Stocks

(Image via Pixabay)

At this point, there should be a comprehensive understanding of what penny stocks are and how to choose them. This chapter will go over the mechanics of buying, selling, bidding, asking, and when and how to do all of those things. If you're still feeling lost, look more into the chart of different stocks. We can't tell you which company to exactly invest in, but you should understand by now how to tell whether or not a certain business is worth it in the end.

Trading stocks is a serious business, and before you start, you have to be prepared. The first step in preparation is knowing that there are going to be moments of failure. There are going to be times that all money is lost, or at least, nothing significant is gained. This is part of the process. There might be a few lucky people that never experience loss, but even the biggest investors have taken a hit every now and then. The important part is staying consistent and having faith that things will eventually pay off. There are a few other important things to remember that we'll go over in this section.

The Rule of 72

The rule of 72 is a common economic concept that isn't inherently just related to stocks. It's a simple way to figure out how long a particular investment might take to double. This is determined by taking a fixed annual rate of interest. If you take the number "72," and divide it by the annual rate of return, an investor can get a rough idea of how many years it might take for an initial investment to duplicate itself.

So, if a dollar is invested at ten percent, then it will take 7.2 years to turn into two dollars. This isn't always necessarily true for everything, but it can certainly help when trying to figure out how long it's going to be until you can count on your investment turning into twice of what you initially put in.

Short Selling

Short selling is when the seller borrows a sale of securities. A short seller only profits when and if a security's price declines. If this doesn't make sense, think of it like how the trader sells to open the position, and they then expect to buy it back later when it has reached a lower price. They are then able to keep the difference as a gain. Short selling may start by someone just making a speculation, but it can also form from the desire to hedge the risk of a certain long position. The risk of a loss when it comes to a short sale is unlimited, so this should only be done by those who are very experienced and familiar with the risks that can come along with it.

A short seller starts this process by borrowing the shares, usually from their broker[19]. The trader then must create a margin account, usually having to pay interest on the borrowed amount, or value of that, to open a short position. When the time comes to close this short position, the trader then buys the share from the market and returns the borrowed money from their broker, or other lenders that gave them the original investment amount.

---

[19] Generally speaking, a broker is a person that will do the buying and selling of goods or assets for those that hire them to do so. When discussing stocks, a broker is the one who will make arrangements and negotiations for the investor. These people will either be workers that directly interact with the investor, or an online service that does the bidding, selling, and buying for others.

Even the biggest experts need brokers to help them short sell, as the process of locating these shares is usually done behind the scenes. Regular opening and closing of a trade can be done normally, but it should be with the help of a broker or another expert. It's a risky process, because there won't always be a return. Sometimes, what's borrowed is completely lost, and since those shares were sold, there's no way of getting them back. The investor is then out of the original amount that was invested.

Determining Risk Level

(Image via Pixabay)

There is always a risk of investing. Sometimes, it can be as tricky as playing the lottery. You'll have a much higher chance of getting something in return when you buy a $5 share, versus a $5 lottery ticket, however. You must determine your own risk level first. If you have $100 to invest, but you also need to feed your family with that money, then the risk is that your family doesn't eat for a week if the money is lost. This risk level is incredibly high, so you just shouldn't invest your money. However, if you have $10 and would otherwise just spend that $10 on clothes, food, or other meaningless purchases, you may as well try turning that $10 into $100 or more.

After your personal risk level is determined, there is a calculation you can actually use to determine whether or not the risk is going to be worth the reward. Take your expected profit and divide it by your maximum risk amount. For example, say you paid $500 for your shares in a company, and it went up to $29, meaning you make $4 per the 200 shares that were purchased. This gives a total reward of $80. This is figured out by dividing $80 (risk) / $500 (reward). The result is 0.16. This should be compared to a 1:1 ratio. The result is .16:1, which is pretty low.

A low risk/reward scenario will usually cause expert investors to walk away, so you should do the same. Don't look at the stock market like a slot machine. Certain risks have to be taken, yes, but you cannot put your money towards chance as often with stocks as you would a gambling machine.

How to Value a Stock

Some might believe that a stock's intrinsic value might be tied directly to the current market price. It's important to remember that this is not always the case. Some people buy into this idea, the concept that all of the information known about a share is being priced into the stock. Using the proper analyzing techniques is important in determining the value of a stock, but there is also a formula that can help you determine what the value of your interested stock might be.

A company's book value can be determined by subtracting liabilities from company assets. All of this information can be found on the company's balance sheet. The book value per share is then found by taking the book value and dividing that by the number of outstanding shares that a particular company has. The last step is to solve for the ratio, which involves dividing the share price by the book value per share. So, the steps go:

1. COMPANY ASSETS – LIABILITIES = BOOK VALUE

2. BOOK VALUE / OUTSTANDING SHARES = BOOK VALUE PER SHARE

3. SHARE PRICE / BOOK VALUE PER SHARE = RATIO

This ratio will then be used to determine whether or not the investment is worth it in the end. Low ratios usually cause investors to run, but those willing to take higher risks may still want to invest in certain companies. It goes without saying that the higher the value of a stock, the higher the return will be in the end. This ratio is important, but it shouldn't be the only thing to consider when deciding whether or not to invest in a particular stock.

Calculating Rates of Return

The next step before deciding whether or not to purchase a share is to calculate the rate of return. By doing this, you can determine how well you might be investing your money. Remember that there is a difference between the total rate of return, and the rate of return in an annual sense. One is how much you're going to be making overall, and the other is just how much is going to be made in a year. While you may see a high number after calculating your rate of return, that doesn't mean you're going to get it all in the next few months. It can take years for investments to actually come through.

Start by subtracting the start value of a stock portfolio from an end value of the same portfolio. This simple calculation can be used at any time and will tell you how much might be made in a year. To find the total rate of return, take the gain and divide it by the starting value. Then add 1.

For example, say that there is a $10,000 gain and a $20,000 starting value. $10,000/$20,000 equals .5, also known as 50 percent. Add a one to this, and the total rate of return becomes 1.5.

Then, take 1 and divide it by the number of years that it might take to achieve this total rate of return. Then, raise one, plus the rate of return (1.5), to the power of 1, then divided by the number of years. So, if the return is going to take 3 years, you would take 1.5 and raise it to the power of .3333 (1/number of years), and the result would be 1.1447.

Once this result is found, subtract one and this will give you your annualized rate of return. 1-1.1447 means 14.47 percent, which is the annualized rate of return. Sometimes, you may have a high rate of return, but you need to compare it to the annualized rate of return to determine if the investment is actually worth it in the end. You might make $1,000 at the end of your investment, but is it really worth that if it takes 5 years to get that $1,000?

Bidding and Asking

Before getting deep into how to bid and ask for certain stock prices, the biggest thing to remember is that stocks go up when there are more buyers than sellers, and oppositely, stocks will go down when more sellers are present than buyers. This is the case in almost any large economic market, including cars and houses. It's the basic idea of supply versus demand.

There is a reason that penny stocks are cheap in the first place. You could put all your money into a penny stock hoping that they will go up just by a dollar, and your $500 will turn into thousands overnight.

A Bid-Ask Spread[20] is in reference to the fact that most of the time, a bid price is below the ask price. Sometimes, the ask and bid become equalized, but for the most part, there is a higher asking price than the bid. This is the Bid-Ask Spread.

Penny stocks can have high bid-ask spreads, which is why many investors choose to put their money towards these. For example, a stock might have last sold for $.60. The current asking price might be $.70, the highest bid being $.55. In this case, the Bid-Ask Spread is %25 of the last purchase price. This large difference mostly affects sellers, though bidders have to wait for the seller to come down as well.

This is when patience is most important. Bidding with a large bid-ask spread means hoping that the seller will come down to meet you. Staying at the lower end of a bid means risking more, as not only do you have just to hope the seller will come down, but you also have to hope that your bid is better than others that have already put their offer in on a share.

---

[20] Bid-Ask Spread is the amount that an asking price differentiates between the bid. Usually, the difference is found between the absolute minimum that the seller wants to sell, and how much the buyer is willing to pay.

Buying

Once it's time to start buying stocks, it's best to open an account with a brokerage service. You won't have to have a broker the entire time you decide to participate in the business of stock, but when you're starting out, it's usually best to have the help of a professional to make sure you're not making any mistakes. You don't have to go to the first person you find on Google, in fact, you can find a broker without even leaving your home. There are online broker services that you can sign up with any time. E-Trade and TD Ameritrade are among the most popular online brokerage services and only require a small deposit upon sign-up.

Another reason using a broker is since penny stocks aren't as regularly monitored as larger stocks. These stocks are more susceptible to scam, so having a professional there helps to uncover any missed clues that an investment might be a scam.

When choosing which order to place, "limit" orders are usually a better option than "market" orders for penny stock trading. This is because you will have a better control over the price of transactions with a limit order. If a market order is used, there is a chance that stock will be purchased at an inflated price. You also might end up selling it too low since other buyers and sellers are placing impracticable bids and ask prices.

Selling

Before buying stock, you have to buy it, but this next step is very important in actually making money. Having stock means nothing if you're not making money by selling it. There are a few different order types when selling your stock.

The first is a market order. This is when the stock is sold at the market price. It is an automatic sale, so the risk is that there's a chance the stock is fluctuating to a number that you wouldn't otherwise sell.

A limit order is one done after a limit price is set. The order only happens if the stock is being traded above, or at the same price, as the limit that was set. For instance, a limit order set at $50 means that the share will only sell at $50 or more, nothing less, even when the market value is lower. This is usually the best option, though it also means that the stock never ends up selling.

A stop-loss order is when a stop price is set much like a limit would. Once stock starts trading at or below your stop price, then the order will execute only then. That means if your lowest price you want to sell is $27, the order will execute as soon as the market price hits $27 or below. This can be risky since it's automatic. So, if your stop price is $27, and the value reaches as low as $22, the order will execute, when really, it was probably better to just sit on that and hope it goes back up.

A stop-limit order is when a stop and a limit price are set. It's a way of combining the previous two concepts. The biggest risk with this among the other methods of selling is that when limits are set, certain shares might not get sold at all.

When actually making a sale, a trade ticket is required. This is usually found online through whichever brokerage service is being used. When the money hits your account is dependent on the terms agreed upon with the brokerage service. Filling out a trade ticket is usually self-explanatory once you have it in front of you.

Volatility

Volatility refers to a statistical measure of how returns are dispersed for any given market index[21], or security. This is measured through the variance or standard deviation of returns (from the market index or security). It's commonly known that the higher a volatility, the higher the risk of security.

Volatility is most thought of when there is a large swing in different directions in securities markets. Falling over a percent

---

[21] Market Index refers to a stock average; the measure of several stocks to determine a certain direction or change in a stock market as a whole.

in either direction will usually mean that a certain market is volatile. A Volatility Index was created by the Chicago Board of Options Exchange and is used as a system of measurement that predicts the volatility in a 30-day range of a certain stock. Many investors use this as a way to determine future "bets." Checking the volatility rating is important before buying, selling, and trading any stocks.

Chapter 5 – Winning Stock Strategies

This chapter will touch on stock strategies that win, though an in-depth look at winning stock strategies will be explored in the book, "Stock Strategies: Learn the Techniques for Build a Sustainable Stock Trading System to Become an Intelligent Investor and Achieve Financial Freedom" from Michael J. Bloomfield.

There's more of a reason than just money why you may get involved in trading stocks. For some people, it can be rather thrilling to give money, get money, and make a big return by simply tossing around some numbers. It's like gambling and can elicit the same feelings you would get from hitting the jackpot on a scratch-off.

There are over 5 million companies that trade publicly in the U.S. alone. This number isn't as high as it used to be, but it still presents investors with a nearly limitless amount of options when it comes to buying and selling stock. This chapter will go on to explore two different popular strategies for buying and selling stock that are already proven winners. Some methods are helpful, but you always have to make sure that they are completely legal. Some ways of trading and selling stocks can be scams, and you don't want to find yourself participating in anything that's less than legal.

Buying on Margin

Buying on Margin basically refers to the idea of borrowing money directly from a broker to purchase certain stock. It's basically a loan from a broker. This is useful for investors to buy more stock than they could on their own. If they're feeling particularly confident with one form of stock, they'll put their money towards that investment with hopefully high returns. The risk of buying on margin[22] is not getting the payoff expected and having to owe brokerage money.

These loans are usually different than other regular loans taken from banks or creditors, as there are fewer restrictions. These loans aren't given as freely as some bank loans, however. There is still interest, and often times, collateral as a security measure. Never buy on margin unless you're absolutely positive that you're going to be able to get the payoff you're expecting.

Buying on margin should only be looked at as a short-term solution. If an investment is held for too long, the return needed to pay it off goes up, meaning less money will be made in the end. You won't always have the option to buy on margin anyways. Most penny stocks can't be bought on margin because of the quick turnaround and high risk that can come along,

---

[22] Buying on margin is the act of borrowing money from a broker to put towards the purchase of stock by an investor. It differs from a regular loan in that there are more assets attached that could be lost. Not many brokers allow those interested in penny stocks to buy on margin.

though some brokers do offer it as an option.

Strategy 1 – Breakout

(Image via Pixabay)

A breakout trading strategy usually involves investors that are actively taking a position in the early stages of a trending share. This strategy might be the beginning moment for some major price movements and expansions of volatility. This strategy is good for many different investors as there is less risk involved than there is with other methods of trading.

A breakout itself involves a stock price that is moving in an undefined level with an increase in the overall volume. The price moves outside the resistance level in a breakout, and the support is not defined either. Someone who is using this plan will enter into a lengthier place after a stock price disrupts above the resistance level, or arrives in a briefer position after the stock interrupts beneath the support level.

Since the stock is being traded beyond the price barrier, there is an increase in volatility, which means that the prices will usually tend in favor of the direction of the breakout. These breakouts then become starting positions that act as future points of volatility increases. This will lead to price swings that are larger than average, which will result in high price trends that become major as well.

Valuation

It's important to remember the valuation[23] of a stock when using a breakout strategy[24]. The support and resistance levels are important because they set the barrier for which a stock will end up breaking out. If using this strategy, the valuation should be consistent when the stock is being traded. The longer there

---

[23] Valuation is the worth of something in an estimation, usually determined by professionals.
[24] Breakout Strategy is a strategy that involves entering into a stock investment once there is a breakout of the price reaching above resistance or below support.

has been a consistent level of support and resistance, the higher the payoff when a breakout actually occurs. Something that is more volatile wouldn't do as well when using a breakout strategy as something that has a higher valuation.

When it comes to evaluating the chart of a stock you might consider using a breakout strategy with - look for symbols like triangles, flags, and channel formations. These patterns, as well as other consistencies seen in various trading charts, will help show a level of constant resistance and support. When this is seen, it's a good indication it will be a good candidate for a breakout strategy trading method.

Growth

Breakout strategies happen quickly, so there isn't always as much growth within them as there would be in other strategies. Instead of steady growth, it's usually a quick jump in value due to the fact that more buyers mean higher prices.

Profitability

To make a profit, it's important to determine when a good exit strategy would be. In a breakout strategy, you would want to make sure that your exit is predetermined so that you don't lose money with this risky method. To find a good exit spot, look at the recent price action of that share. If it was last purchased at 4 points, use that as a standard or target to help protect your investments forward once the breakout occurs.

You could also figure out the average of recent price swings and use this as a point for your target price to pull out your investment. Before going in with this strategy, you have to determine what your goal price is to sell and stick to this to ensure that there are no losses.

You also have to keep in mind the fact that unfortunately, you just might end up with some unfortunate losses with this strategy. To prepare for this, you have to know when it's time to give up and exit with your loss. It can be hard to lose money, but you still have to be ready to do so and just pull your investments before losing even more money than you already did. Many people would only prefer to hold out and wait for that investment to get higher again, but sometimes, this doesn't come, and all money is lost in the end.

Strategy 2 – Momentum

Another great strategy to use is the momentum strategy. This is mostly used with day trading and highly associated with stocks that are actually moving. Each and every day in the stock market, there is almost always at least one stock that moves between 15-35 percent, sometimes even more.

A momentum strategy aims to find these stocks that are actually moving to choose when to make the right move. The most important thing needed for stocks that are approached with the momentum strategy are stocks that are actually moving. Those that seem to be going side to side with little volatility are not ones that are good candidates for the momentum strategy.

There are a few other things that are important to consider when choosing stocks for the momentum strategy. These stocks should have less than one hundred million shares. This is because you don't want as many investors catching on and using the momentums strategy, or else it becomes pointless.

Trends, breaking news, and general discussion about a company are also important for a momentum stock. If there's a PR announcement or press release on a certain product, this is probably the time to use a momentum strategy with that stock.

Valuation

Valuation is important to consider with this strategy, as well as all other strategies. There should be no resistance nearby for a stock's daily chart. When looking at the valuation for this strategy versus the last one, think of looking at the chart the opposite way you did for a breakout strategy.

Growth

When it comes to finding a consistent level of growth with momentum trading, it's important to trade with a lower profit-loss ratio. One of 2:1 is usually standard to follow when considering a momentum trading strategy. So, if you have $2, your potential for a profit should be $4. To see growth with this trading strategy, there must be a balance of risk. Calculating risk is very important with this strategy, as there is a little more at stake than there was with the breakout method.

Profitability

To achieve high profitability from the momentum strategy, this method must be started in the morning. Not all spikes occur in the morning, but it's still important to keep up with what's going on early in the day to catch a good time to invest.

To profit, these must be sold the same day they were purchased. Momentum stocks have to be watched very closely as well. Momentum strategies require quick action, and missing a step just once, no matter how small, can cause serious losses if serious investments were made, of course.

Trading Styles

The past two sections went over popular trading strategies that many investors, even the most successful, will use to have a high profitability return. There are a few other strategies that a new investor can adopt that will very much help make money in the end.

This final section will discuss the trading styles that you are most likely going to come across. You can use these yourself, or you can just make yourself knowledgeable to avoid falling for someone else's tricks that might cause you to lose money in the end.

Trading styles are mostly determined by how long someone plans on keeping their investment. Some trading styles work for those who want to pull out right away while there are other methods in which you can keep your investments for days, weeks, or months at a time. To find the right trading style that works for you, make sure that you are considering how long you plan to keep your investment.

Another large factor in determining trading style is the timing of your entry as well. Sometimes, it might not be the greatest time in the market for one strategy, while other strategies require very specific moments of action.

The frequency of the trades is also very important when

figuring out when a person should invest or pull their shares. This isn't as important as the other two, but together, these three key elements are important to consider when choosing which trading style works best for your shares.

Scalp Styles

Scalping strategies are ones that occur all in the same day. This method is much different from any other style, and it's very important for anyone using this strategy to constantly keep up with stocks at all times throughout the day.

Those using scalping styles will always consider technical analysis versus fundamental analysis. Usually, there isn't even enough time to do an in-depth fundamental analysis of a particular stock. This method is very hard because it requires someone to be watching stocks all day, from morning to night. This is a ton of discipline that not all people are ready for when they first begin stock trading. It's still important to remember that there will be plenty of people in the market who are ready to use these scalping strategies.

Profits from scalp strategies are taken after even the smallest of price changes. There has to be a strict entry and exit strategy with this scalping method to ensure maximum profits and minimum losses. Scalping happens very quick and involves taking profits, no matter how little, at quick rates. The reason it's successful is because there is a ton of little profit versus one long run for a certain stock. Many people who decide to trade penny stocks will decide to use some sort of scalping style to ensure that they are getting as much for their bronze coin as possible. Not everyone will be capable of this challenging method, but it's certainly one to consider when a high profit is desired.

Day Styles

Besides scalping, there are other day styles of trading stock that should be considered. This involves an analysis of a certain stock on a daily, or at a maximum, weekly basis to determine certain trends of the market. Those who use day styles might automate their orders and set them based around daily trends. This is an easier method than scalping as you can still work or do other things as the numbers fluctuate, instead of being forced to remain glued to the screen.

Though this method is popular and works for money, it can still produce results of a loss. It's important to set points that won't produce as much of a profit loss when automating day to day orders. Just as risky as loss is, great growth is also achievable, so it's important to remember that the two go hand in hand. Some people that frequently use day trading style are also seen as gamblers in the stock market world.

Buying on margin is a popular method of purchasing for those who are using this method as well.

Swing Styles

Swing styles involve traders that are looking at the swing in a chart, hoping to catch something as it goes back and forth. Think of the fluctuation as a string with a cat toy at the end. The traders are the cats trying to catch something at high points where they can achieve the greatest growth potential. These styles can be applied daily, though there are certainly methods that involve investing weeks of time into a stock as well.

The profits are usually smaller targets, around %10. Though it might take a couple of weeks to swing just right, the actual trade is between 5-10 days. The large returns are usually a result of smaller wins that add together to make a larger sum.

Position Styles

Though there are many strategies you can choose to trade stocks, the final one we will discuss are position styles of trading. This involves someone who has a long-term position with a stock, usually weeks or more. These traders don't look at short fluctuations because they have more concerns over the long-term results of their investments, knowing that though each small battle isn't one, the war will be theirs in the end.

These position traders use fundamental analysis more than any other method discussed so far. They won't look at trading charts as much and will instead put a focus on what's trending in the next month that could bring them large returns. They usually don't buy on margin either as they need more long-term investments, and this isn't always the best option.

Those using position styles know that trends have expiration dates, and they're very good at looking at each point in a trend's lifestyle. They use this to their advantage to make larger gains. If you feel more comfortable with a fundamental analysis versus a technical one, and you are more interested in long-term gains than short risks, consider position styles.

Chapter 6 – The Basket

Once stock investments have been made, protecting them is absolutely crucial. You can't put all your effort into learning how to understand, buying, and selling stocks just to abandon them once you have started trading. To ensure you're getting the maximum return, do everything in your power to protect your stocks.

There is a level of ruthlessness in the market that we need to protect ourselves from as investors. The title of this chapter refers to the Warren Buffett[25] motto that revolves around the idea of not putting all your eggs in one basket.

If you are not aware of all the ways that you can wind up losing your money, you will be more susceptible to scams and schemes in the end. The more you know about what can go wrong, the less likely you'll have to experience something actually going wrong.

While many penny stocks can be found in lower caliber markets such as pink sheets and OTC, it's a better idea to try to stick to penny stocks that are often traded through the AMEX[26], OTC-BB, and Nasdaq.

---

[25] Warren Buffet is one of the wealthiest and most respected businessmen in the world, known for being the "Oracle of Omaha," as well as an investment guru. He holds a net worth of $86 billion.
[26] The American Stock Exchange, which emerged in the 18th century as the American trading market was developing.

You should never buy stocks based on some sort of "tip" or idea from someone that you know, no matter how close you two are. While there are certainly some people that have great opinions and may even know more than you about stocks, you should still try and do your own research as often as possible to avoid running into any issues. What works for someone else isn't always going to be the answer to reaching your own goals.

Avoid free stock altogether. Just as there's a reason penny stocks are so cheap, there's an even bigger reason why these stocks are free. It's in your best interest to never get caught up in free stocks, no matter how tempting that $0 price tag might be.

No matter whose story you've heard of success, you never want to follow directly in someone else's footsteps. While there are plenty of people that have made tons of money from different methods, you can't expect to get the exact same results by doing the exact same things as them. There are certainly going to be factors and different stipulations that have caused them to reach their success, and their path to fortune could be yours to a financial crisis.

Diversification

Diversification[27] refers to the mixing of different investments among one investor. This is the method of putting your eggs in different baskets to make sure that nothing ends up cracked or broken. If one does, then at least you have different eggs in different baskets. A perfect portfolio includes a diverse one with many small investments rather than a huge one. While sometimes putting all your money in one place can equal a higher return, it's better to try and get as much as you can from smaller investments to ensure that if something doesn't win, your losses won't be as big.

This risk management technique ensures that you're going to get the maximum from your money with as little risk as possible. It makes sense in concept, and there are certainly studies that prove that this is a successful way for investors to protect their money.

Diversification also involves investing in foreign trades as well, as they might be less likely to be affected should something at a national level happens that hurts your investments. Some financial crisis is unavoidable even on a global level, but the

---

[27] Diversification in stock, is the act of spreading investments throughout many different companies instead of just one. By practicing diversification, a person has a better chance of ensuring that they don't suffer from a massive loss that they might have endured if they had put all their money into one company.

more diversified your investments, the more likely you're going to be protected if something does end up going wrong.

Portfolio Management

To ensure that your investments are going to do well, have a proper portfolio management. Investing in penny stocks means staying incredibly organized to ensure that you don't run into any problems. You want to make sure that your investments are well laid out and easily understandable so that you are prepared for anything to happen, whether it's good or bad.

A good portfolio management includes one that knows the strengths and weaknesses in each and every investment. Managing your portfolio well means seeing all the opportunities that your investments are capable of, while also acknowledging the various threats you might run into as well.

You also have to treat all of your assets differently. Some strategies might not work with other trades, while others are consistently looked at the same. Know that your diverse set of investments also have to be treated in a different way. Appreciate the uniqueness in each and every stock to ensure they are being properly managed.

Rebalancing is a method that involves returning a particular portfolio back to its original target allocations. These allocations should be looked at in annual intervals. By rebalancing your portfolio, you are making sure to stick to your goals while overlooking anything bad that could happen as well as checking in on all the various threats your portfolio is experiencing.

The Mindset

One of the most important things for a trader to have is a mind that's open to interpretation to ensure maximum potential from an investment. Sometimes, you might want to just look at the numbers and figure out what a good investment might be based strictly on what you see on your trading chart. What's more important than numbers is your mindset. Are you going to be able to do what it takes to make money? Are you going to let fear, anxiety, passion, and desire cloud your judgment?

Will you be able to mentally recover if you end up losing a ton of money? This is a part that some of us have to be prepared for. If we do end up with a loss, there's a desire to either quit and never return to stocks, or a feeling of wanting to risk more in the hopes of a greater return. Sometimes, our only option is just to accept that we've lost some money. We can't always put out a ton more money trying to recover from our losses, as this might end up making us lose even more in the end. There are some important things to ask yourself before getting into the trading business.

Will you have enough discipline when it comes to sticking to your trading rules? Sometimes, gamblers hit a streak and feel like they should keep going with their bets until they hit a big payout. This isn't always going to produce the results that you want in trading stocks, however. Hitting a good streak doesn't mean you should spontaneously bet more. Alternatively, hitting a low point isn't an indication that you should try to make up for those losses or pullout forever. You have to stick to your goals to ensure that you don't end up with even more losses in the end.

Do you have the judgment it takes to know when a deal is good or not? There are going to be times you might get tricked into putting your time and money towards an investment because of all the bells and whistles around it, and not the actual real situation of that particular investment. Do you have what it takes to look at a share and know whether or not you're being tricked into buying into something? You have to stay disciplined with your beliefs and ideologies, or else you can really get tricked into some seriously bad things in this business. We'll discover more risks in later chapters of this book. For now, make sure you're in the right mindset to start trading. This isn't a game of poker. It's really money being traded and isn't always dependent upon chance alone.

Chapter 7 – The Darkside of the Stock Market

(Image via Pixabay)

Though trading penny stocks can be exhilarating, it isn't all fun and games when it comes to sending around different amounts of money. It can be a very serious business and shouldn't be taken lightly. This chapter will go over the dark side of the market and ways that users can be tricked and scammed out of their money. This chapter is not at all meant to make you fearful or scared of trading stocks. Not everyone will experience what it means to lose their money to a scam. It's important to know what issues a person might run into, so they can be completely avoided, and you'll never have to worry about falling victim to any particular scam or trick.

What's in this chapter isn't meant to scare anyone away from the market, only ensure that those most curious are aware of the potential risks. Some people see penny stocks as very risky and dangerous, and this can be true. This is only because of the low price tag, so many people think that they don't have to be as aware of stocks as those that might be trading blue-chip shares. Some people see that they can buy stocks for less than $10, so they buy a lot not realizing that they could end up losing a ton of money in the end. Penny stocks can be risky, but only because so many people don't do the research that is required for these stocks.

Many people also see the consistent fluctuation in price of these stocks, thinking that they can make a ton of money if these fluctuate high. The chances of this happening without a lot of work are very low, and not everyone realizes that they are just as at risk with low fluctuations as they have the chance of hitting one that's high.

Notable Case of Scammers

In as recent as 2014, a money manager from Connecticut was arrested, along with seven other people, after being caught participating in a large pump-and-dump scheme caught by federal authorities. They managed to steal millions of dollars from a variety of people that had invested in penny stocks.

The money manager, Abraxas J. Discala, who goes by A.J., was the CEO of a Rowayton-based OmniView Capital. This manager was best known for marrying *Sopranos* actress Jamie-Lynn Sigler. It seems he let her onscreen family's character bleed into his real life too much as he found himself in the middle of a stock scheme.

A.J., among his other accomplices, manipulated microcap stocks belonging to Code Smart. They discussed their schemes through texts and calls, federal authorities revealing eventually that their scheme started by purchasing 3 million shares at 2.3 cents per piece. They eventually implemented a 2 for-1 stock split, eventually showing six million shares that were shared through falsified SEC files. What they did was incredibly illegal, and we'll discuss this pump and dump scheme further.

High Risks

Penny stocks are often seen as higher risk investments since they aren't as monitored as other stocks. This is because most don't see the point since they hold little value. Others see this as a chance to take advantage of those looking for a quick buck. What's most important is ensuring that you won't run into any issues of being cheated or scammed. You have to make sure that you're well-aware and educated of all the risks before going into this business. You can still find penny stocks on Nasdaq, which is better than using other forms of finding penny stocks.

Since these aren't as regulated, you might find that you bought something that's actually worthless. Avoiding illiquid[28] stocks is also important to make sure that you don't get scammed twice. At first, you might buy something that's less, you might not realize that even a dollar can move the market, which will result in you paying out a higher price. Then, when the time comes to sell, you might end up feeling the pressure to sell shares at lower prices because there seems to be less people that are in the market.

Manipulations in the Market

For scammers, criminals, and other traders that are looking to take advantage of others through stocks, penny stocks are the place they go to. That is why you have to be very aware of manipulations in the market before getting into different purchasing schemes that could end up wiping your savings before you know it. The people that get taken advantage of are simply those that don't know what's going on. That's why the

---

[28] Illiquid assets are those that cannot be exchanged for cash, at least not so easily. In terms of a stock market, this term refers to one that has a lower number of participants and volume of activity.

more informed you are, the better you'll be able to protect yourself from various forms of scams or trickery.

Sometimes, just because a price went up half a cent, some feel as though this isn't a big loss. This is how people get tricked, however. A tenth of a penny can quickly turn into a full penny, and people end up losing a ton of money.

Thinly traded stocks have the power to manipulate others. It appears that when there are fewer shares traded, it's easier for a bunch of buyers coming in to change the value of a stock. No matter how many shares are being sold, however, they will still be affected when even the smallest purchase is made.

Another reason many investors fall into scams is because they are too trusting of the legitimacy of certain stocks. There is no amount of research on stocks that is too much, so it's important to know that there still might be stocks out there that can be very much fake, or not legitimate, and could cause you to lose money. Always do fundamental analysis of all companies before investing. You don't have to use this fundamental analysis as your basis of when or how much to invest, but it's still important to use to make sure that you're not buying into something fake.

Short and Distort

Short and Distort is a scam in which certain shareholders will short a stock, then spread rumors about a stock to drive down the price. These rumors are unsubstantiated and only used as a way for people to get the price of their shares way down. This is done by those that work online who are able to use their power to influence others into believing their lies and manipulations. By lowering prices, many other people will try and sell their stocks, and those with automated order requirements will quickly lose their stocks, allowing others to swoop in and take these cheaper prices. Then, when the price goes back up, those who spread the rumors in the first place will end up making a huge profit.

This type of scam is illegal and will result in serious fines and penalties. Lies spread on the internet will always be discovered, so before basing a major trading decision on a news story you heard, make sure that you check the sources. Sometimes, even reputable news sources will end up reporting on a false story, so don't do anything unless you're 100% certain that your stocks are rapidly losing money.

Pump and Dump

A pump and dump scam is when an investor promotes the stock, they hold only to sell it once the price rises. This is why following tips and trends can be dangerous. The stockholder won't show that they own the stock, usually disguising their names or using a fake company to invest. They'll end up spreading the word that this is what's rising and what's most important on the market to put your money towards. People will rush to purchase, causing the price to rise rapidly.

Companies that are highly liquid can cause the hype to rise, usually ones with sharp movement as well that can be traded over the counter. This is done for a short-term gain and is most, of the time, very illegal. A good rule of thumb to follow to rule out a pump and dump scheme is to ask yourself if it's too good to be true. Most of the time, things that are too good to be true end up being untrue in the end, simple as that.

Certainly, don't listen to anyone you don't know about the rise of a stock, and even those you do know and trust around you might be falling for a pump and dump scheme as well. These tricks work because of others' willingness to be involved, so it's best to avoid rumors of rising stocks altogether.

Insider Trading

Insider trading refers to the practice of someone purchasing stocks in companies they have other investments in, based on information that only they have. A notable case of this is Martha Stewart and ImClone, which ended up getting her in serious trouble. Insider trading isn't always involved with trading stock and is sometimes involved in corporate espionage[29].

Insider trading hasn't always been illegal, but it's certainly a practice that needs to be regulated now. If someone doesn't share information on their own company or one they are involved with, and keeps knowledge away from the general public, they can continually gain/avoid losses while others are still suffering. If this weren't regulated, the stock market and economic consistencies would be much different today.

Insider trading might still occur but it isn't the largest risk to those wanting to trade penny stocks. It's still something to be aware of. Luckily, Section 16 of the Securities and Exchange Act

---

[29] Corporate espionage refers to the practice of investigating other businesses, mostly competitors, to gain an upper hand on other companies. These missions are covert in nature, sometimes even involving illegal practices to gain a particular intel.

of 1934[30] protects traders.

Chapter 8 – Taking Action with Penny Stocks

The most important part of this entire process is actually taking action. It can be scary for some people to get started. They might fear what could happen when they begin to invest. If you never try, then you'll never end up making any money. No matter how scary it might feel to start putting money towards different investments, it's necessary to make sure that you're going to do the thing that's going to fulfill your goals and dreams.

Opening Your Account and Making Your First Trade

Once you have the right knowledge, have done the right research, and have gotten yourself in the correct mindset to start trading, it's time to open your account. You can do this with a broker, which is certainly recommended for your first time. There are some interactive brokers, such as Trade Monster, TD Ameritrade, and Options Xpress that will help you get started in creating your account that you're going to be using to trade.

After you've opened your account and done your proper

---

[30] Section 16 of the Securities and Exchange Act of 1934 states that any owner, whether they are an officer or director of a company, are required to report if they hold more than ten percent of any beneficial ownership.

research and analysis, it's time to make your first trade! Remember when evaluating costs that you're likely going to have to pay a brokerage fee. As you become more experienced, you might not need one, but you will need one in the beginning just to make sure you're not making any rookie mistakes. There might also be a minimum account balance that is required to open a penny stock with a broker. While some people choose to do things on their own to avoid these fees, it's important to remember you might end up losing more money as an inexperienced trader than you would have had you just invested in a broker in the first place.

Tools Needed

The most important tool in trading stocks is a reliable internet connection. A few decades ago it wasn't needed, but now, everyone's on the internet. To make sure you're keeping up with different stocks and quick changes, staying online is going to be an important part of ensuring that you're consistently making the right investment choices.

In addition to your internet, make sure that you have a secured network and fraudulent protection so that no one can hack into your accounts. You don't want to make yourself vulnerable online to anyone looking to scam you out of your trades or money.

The other important tool you'll need to invest is your money! While buying on margin is an option for many people, you don't want to start off your trading empire with borrowed money. This is a practice that should be reserved for more experienced traders who won't have to risk losing out on a large amount of money. When it comes to investing in stocks, start with your own money to make sure you're off to a great beginning.

Practicing with a Demo

It is highly recommended to anyone getting into stocks to first use a demo before getting started. Some people are very eager to start making money, and you could double your money within just a week! This will never be done, however, if you don't first start with a trading demo that can help you catch different mistakes and learn other tricks that will help you become a better trader.

Not only will this help you get to know how to trade stocks better, but you can also make sure that you're building confidence. Some people miss out on certain opportunities because they were too afraid to take the risk. If you make sure that you have the confidence to do what you think is right, you'll be less likely to make a mistake in the end.

It's also a great way to become familiar with different trading software. Stocks can be complicated, so not everyone will be able to walk away from this reading completely confident and ready to make their first trade. We would love if that were possible, but in reality, there is going to be more practice required to start trading. A surgeon wouldn't be able to read a book and then perform their first surgery. Practice makes perfect!

Finding a Broker

Before getting started with a broker, make sure that they deal with penny stocks. Not everyone will help you trade penny stocks, and some require more of an upfront investment if you do decide to trade these lower priced shares. Unfortunately, just like there are in the stock market, there are some brokers that are scam artists looking to take your money. Be sure your broker is reputable and certified, especially when finding one online.

Choosing a reputable broker is extremely important. If the broker is a scam, it doesn't matter how good someone might be in the market-they will fail anyway. Choosing a broker is an investment in itself, and though some people would rather do things on their own, they still need to make sure that they are getting the help from someone who knows what they're doing.

When looking for a good broker, make sure your broker of choice is regulated and accredited. Even if someone you know and trust recommends a broker, be sure to check them out. They might end up just being that person's cousin that just got started in the market. You wouldn't want to find yourself getting help from someone that might end up losing your money in the end.

It's also important to be sure they have a dispute resolution policy[31] you agree with, as well as reputable reviews that you trust. Their leverage[32] should be at a decent level as well to ensure that you're going to get the money you deserve in a way that makes you feel comfortable.

Setting Goals

Setting goals is an incredibly important part of this process. Start by deciding what your personal goals are, not attached to any monetary number. Do you want to make enough money to pay off your student loans? Maybe you're trying to come up

---

[31] A resolution policy is a broker's specific manual that will layout terms of privacy, conflict and dispute monitoring, crisis management, and other important terms that need to be laid out before entering an agreement.
[32] In reference to finding a broker, leverage refers to how much-borrowed shares a someone would allow, usually to buy on margin.

with the down payment of a car or a house. Perhaps you even want to try to get into stocks, so you can quit the job you hate and work from home as little as possible. Whatever your reason might be, figure out on a personal level why you're choosing stocks.

From there, start to set monetary goals. Do you need to make $20,000 in two years? Maybe you're aiming as high as to make $1,000,000 within the next five. Whatever your goal might be, make sure it's based on something realistic that you can get into in a safe way. If you set a high goal that requires a lot of risks, you might set yourself back in the end of it all. Be sure that you're realistic with your goals, while also setting them high enough to the point that your costs get covered.

Chapter 9 – Tips, Tricks, and Common Mistakes

At this point, you should have a basic understanding of what penny stocks are, why you would choose them, how to get started, how to find a broker and all of the dangers that you might run into when starting to trade with penny stocks.

In this last chapter, we'll cover some important tips, tricks, and mistakes that you should keep with you on your journey towards making money with penny stocks. Not everyone is going to find immediate success, but these tips can certainly help you get closer to achieving your goals.

Expert Tips and Uncommon Tricks

Companies with strong balance sheets are going to be among the greatest of those that you can invest in. By finding a company with a strong balance sheet, you can ensure that they have a very strong financial strength, meaning you're less likely to run into the issue of the stock crashing.

Finding a company with an LTD[33] that has less than 50% of shareholder equity is also a good thing to look for when investing. A company with a high amount of debt should have at least twice their amount of debt in shareholder equity. Of

---

[33] LTD refers to a limited company that is privately held.

course, the lower the better, as it ensures the company will not buckle underneath itself.

Profitable companies are the ones to invest in as well. This might seem obvious, but some people see the trading charts of a less profitable company and decide to put their money in that direction. This isn't always going to help out in the long run, however. When choosing a profitable company. Analyze whether the shares are public or private. Companies with private shares are looking for long-term investments, so they're not going to be as focused on profit, meaning you might not get as much for your money.

Many people will look to pink sheets for their penny stocks but try to stick to higher quality markets such as NASDAQ. By doing this, you're already improving your odds of success and lowering the chances that you might miss out on a certain amount of money.

Common Mistakes

Some things in life require making your own mistakes, but trading stock is more concerned about learning from others. When there's a high amount of money and risk involved, it's usually best to be aware of the common pitfalls of investors as possible to ensure that you don't end up making these mistakes yourself. Too many people find themselves in the path of losing money because they were too quick to get started or thought that they would never be the ones to end up falling for different schemes and scams.

The biggest mistake new investors make is thinking that they know enough. There is never too much you can know about stocks, and even the biggest and longest investors are still learning new important tips that change the way they move their money. Those that trade penny stocks are most susceptible to running into problems resulting in a lack of awareness because many assume that the low price means there's low risk. If you're not careful enough, you could quickly lose your savings on penny stock alone.

Another common mistake is going in with no strategy. You can't always predict the future, but you can make sure that you're not allowing yourself to go in unprepared. Knowing about different strategies can help make sure that you end up choosing the right one. Your strategy might change up a bit once the bidding and selling actually starts, but for the most part, you should make sure that you're doing your best to follow your strategy and stick to the predetermined rules you put in place before the trading started.

Conclusion

"Rule No. 1: Never lose money. Rule No. 2: Never forget rule No.1" - Warren Buffett

You should know by reaching this point in the book, investing in penny stocks isn't easy. It's not going to be a process that happens overnight, and some might run into some loss before they even make $1.

However, with the proper tools, dedication, commitment, and knowledge, anyone is capable of making their first trade. If you have made it this far, you should be proud of yourself! Education is the first and most important step in the right direction towards gaining financial freedom with penny stocks.

Your next step will be to set up your account with a broker to get the process started. It can be risky, but it should not be something that is avoided. Sometimes, fear is what can help drive a decision towards the right direction!

Popular and Requested Questions

1. How much money do I need to get started?

    This can have a few different answers. The amount of money needed is dependent upon which brokerage service you choose. Some might require a minimum deposit, but others don't require anything at all. The only amount needed is what the smallest share costs in the company you wish to invest. Some people might buy only one share for $.01 or less, while others buy hundreds of shares worth $500. The only required amount is how much you're willing to invest and how much you're willing to lose.

2. What kind of stocks should I buy?

    Start with stocks associated with brands and companies you love. The more you know about a business, the better you'll be able to predict the fundamentals that might affect the price of the stock. Always make sure that the stock purchased is reputable.

3. How do I know when to buy?

    To know when to make your first purchase, you have to come up with your strategy. Once this is done, you can then decide if you're going to invest when trends are rising, or there is a breakout of an otherwise consistent pattern.

4. How do I know how to sell?

Sell when it feels right to pull out as a price is rising. The goal is to sell when the price is the highest, but sometimes, investors might miss this. If a stock is dropping in price, it's also important to determine when to know to cut losses, and when to stick it out in the chance that the price might rise again. Technical and fundamental analyses of the stock will help determine when to sell.

5. Are buying/selling penny stocks safe?

Yes. The reason some people feel as though penny stocks aren't safe is that they aren't regulated. If you know what you're doing and don't make poor decisions when investing, they can be completely safe.

6. Is buying/selling penny stocks worth it?

Yes, but only to those who are willing to put in the time and dedication, it takes to see a return. If the commitment of time, the use of patience, and pennies on the dollar are worth growing to you, then yes, penny stocks are worth it.

7. Is selling penny stocks legal?

Selling penny stocks is legal. Schemes like "pump and dump" or insider trading are not, however.

8. Can I become a millionaire with penny stocks?

Not everyone that invests in penny stocks is a millionaire. There is no guarantee that millions will be made from penny stocks either. Some people have managed to turn their investment of penny stocks into a multi million-dollar fortune, however. It's all up to you.

9. What is the best strategy for buying penny stocks?

The best strategy is one that is planned, with strict buying and selling points. Some people might find success with buying on a whim, but a planned strategy is always better.

10. What's the biggest mistake investors make?

The biggest mistake investors make is lacking the knowledge it takes to ensure that a sale is legitimate, as well as having a proper strategy to enter and exit a trade.

11. Do I need a broker?

> A broker is not legally required, but it is highly encouraged, especially for first time traders.

12. How long does it take to make money?

> Some transactions can be done within a day, however, when funds are deposited depends upon the service being used. Money is not guaranteed, however, so more research is encouraged before beginning an investment.

13. What are the requirements for buying/selling penny stock?

> The only requirement is the money it takes to purchase a share. Everything else is up to you!

Glossary

AMEX – The American Stock Exchange, which emerged in the 18th century as the American trading market was developing.

Bid-Ask Spread – the amount that an asking price differentiates between the bid. Usually, the difference is found between the absolute minimum that the seller wants to sell, and how much the buyer is willing to pay.

Blue Chip – this term refers to high-quality products and services. Blue Chip stock is among the highest priced, but also the highest quality, stock that a person could buy. It is derivative of the highest chip in poker, the blue-chip.

Breakout Strategy – A strategy that involves entering into a stock investment once there is a breakout of the price reaching above resistance or below support.

Broker – generally speaking, a broker is a person who will do the buying and selling of goods or assets for those that hire them to do so. When discussing stocks, a broker is the one who will make arrangements and negotiations for the investor. These people will either be workers who directly interact with the investor, or an online service that does the bidding, selling, and buying for others.

Buying on Margin – This is the act of borrowing money from a broker to put towards the purchase of stock by an investor. It differs from a regular loan in that there are more assets attached that could be lost. Not many brokers allow those interested in penny stocks to buy on margin.

Candle Patterns – refers to a movement seen among trading charts in which the pattern represents a candlestick. These movements might have the ability to predict a market movement, helping investors know whether or not they are making a good decision.

Corporate Espionage – refers to the practice of investigating other businesses, mostly competitors, to gain the upper hand on other companies. These missions are covert in nature, sometimes even involving illegal practices to gain a particular intel.

Diversification – in stock, the act of spreading investments throughout many different companies instead of just one. By practicing diversification, a person has a better chance of ensuring that they don't suffer from a massive loss that they might have endured if they had put all their money into one company.

Dividend – refers to the payment made from a corporation to the shareholders of a certain stock. Sometimes, stock shares might be distributed to shareholders in place of a cash payment.

ETF – refers to an exchange-traded fund. An ETF tracks the

stock index, bonds, assets, and commodities. It is different than other mutual funds in that shares are traded as if they were common stock in a market exchange.

Earnings Ratio – sometimes referred to as a P/E ratio. This is the amount of money that one will invest into a stock versus how much money they will earn per share. This ratio is important in evaluating companies as well as determining whether or not an investment is worth it.

FAANG – this refers to Facebook, Apple, Amazon, Netflix, and Google. These five top companies make up one-eighth of the wealth on the New York Stock Exchange.

FINRA – The Financial Industry Regulatory Authority. This is an independent security firm that conducts regulatory business in the United States. They are responsible for regulating securities, which refer to the financial industries that are traded among different free stock markets.

Fundamental Analysis – this is a method of evaluating a stock to determine the value. Fundamental analysis includes looking at a company's fundamental pars, such as status, marketing, affiliates, and other relevant parts of the company to determine the value. This differs from a technical analysis, which looks more into the numbers.

Growth Stock – refers to stock that doesn't have a profit, and instead increases in capital value.

Illiquid – assets that cannot be exchanged for cash, at least not so easily. In terms of a stock market, this term refers to one that has a lower number of participants and volume of activity.

Income Stocks – income stocks are those that pay more regularly than any other form of stocks. They often increase in dividends as well. They don't require as much initial investment either.

Insider Trading – an illegal practice that involves trades made by an investor that has knowledge made confidential in favor of that investor.

LTD – a limited company that is privately held.

Leverage – in reference to finding a broker, this refers to how much-borrowed shares a someone would allow, usually to buy on margin.

Liquify – in reference to something that can easily be traded for cash.

Market Index – a stock average; the measure of several stocks to determine a certain direction or change in a stock market as a whole.

Market Fundamental – refers to the basic fundamental qualities of a particular company. Fundamentals include looking at a business's operation, management, media attention, customers, need, and other basic traits that make up a company.

NYSE – "New York Stock Exchange," the largest stock market in the world, located in New York City.

Nasdaq – a method of using a quick and computerized way to trade stock. It was developed in 1971 by the National Association of Securities Dealers.

OTCBB – stands for over-the-counter bulletin board, which is a digital trading service, also provided by NASD, in which investors and traders can have consistent quotes of different stock, giving insight into up-to-date stock information.

Penny Stock – stock that is valued at less than a dollar per share.

Peter Lynch – one of the most successful investors in the world. He is a former manager of the Magellan Fund, and has become a millionaire philanthropist who inspires many other investors.

Pink Sheet – a publication created by the National Quotation Bureau. It is released on a daily basis and exhibits OTC stock bids and ask prices, as well as the investors that are doing the exchanging.

Pump and Dump – A securities fraud involving the artificial inflation of the price of a stock to sell stock that was cheaply purchased at a higher price. This is usually done through false statements and positive misleading to give the illusion of something that has more value.

Rebalancing – This is done when an investor needs to either buy or sell assets to make sure they're maintaining a level of asset allocation.

Resistance and Support – Also referred to as the "ceiling" of stock prices, as these are the points on a stock chart that are used to keep the market price from increasing. Support would be the lowest point.

Resolution Policy – a broker's specific manual that will layout terms of privacy, conflict and dispute monitoring, crisis management, and other important terms that need to be laid out before entering an agreement.

S&P 500 Index – an index of the 500 largest U.S. companies that are publicly traded. It is organized by the market value and is market-capitalization-weighted.

SEC – Securities and Exchange Commission; an agency of the U.X. Government that is responsible for monitoring securities transactions, as well as the activities of investors and traders in the attempt to prevent scams, fraud, and any other illegal activity.

Section 16 of the Securities and Exchange Act of 1934 – states that any owner, whether they are an officer or director of a company, are required to report if they hold more than ten percent of any beneficial ownership.

Stock – a subscription of shares of a company that raise a corporation's capital.

Stock Market – the exchange of stock.

Technical Analysis – an analysis of a company looking at the numbers rather than the fundamental aspects of what makes up that business.

The Global Stock Market – a place where markets and exchanges that involve buying and selling stock occurs on an international level.

Valuation – the worth of something in an estimation, usually determined by professionals.

Value Stock – company shares in which the fundamental aspects are less than competitors, usually determined after all aspects of value are analyzed.

Volatility – a change that is rapid and unpredicted, more often than not, in a way that will have negative results.

Warren Buffett – one of the wealthiest and most respected businessmen in the world, known for being the "Oracle of Omaha," as well as an investment guru. He holds a net worth of $86 billion.

Notes from the reader

36312144R00058

Printed in Poland
by Amazon Fulfillment
Poland Sp. z o.o., Wrocław